THE SCIENCE BEHIND...

SOCCER

ALIX WOOD

Enslow PUBLISHING

Unfortunately, accidents can happen during any sport. Wear suitable clothing and follow all safety advice. Do not try the skills in this book without supervision from a trained adult expert.

Published in 2023 by Enslow Publishing, LLC
2544 Clinton Street
Buffalo, NY 14224

Produced for Enslow Publishing by Alix Wood Books
Designed and illustrated by Alix Wood
Edited by Eloise Macgregor

Photo credits: 5, 7, 11, 13, 15, 19, 25, © AdobeStock Images; All illustrations © Alix Wood

Cataloging-in-Publication Data
Names: Wood, Alix.
Title: Soccer / Alix Wood.
Description: New York : Enslow Publishing, 2023. | Series: The science behind... | Includes glossary and index.
Identifiers: ISBN 9781978533158 (pbk.) | ISBN 9781978533172 (library bound) |
ISBN 9781978533189 (ebook)
Subjects: LCSH: Soccer--Juvenile literature.| Sports sciences--Juvenile literature.
Classification: LCC GV943.25 W66 2023 | DDC 796.334--dc23

Printed in the United States of America

CPSIA compliance information: Batch #CWENS23: For further information contact Enslow Publishing LLC at 1-800-398-2504.

Welcome, Zink!

Zink wants to join the soccer team. He is really excited! But Zink is a robot, and that can cause some problems. Robots need really clear instructions. Zink's teammates will need to break every soccer skill down into simple scientific steps to teach him how to play! He's hoping his new teammates are good at science as well as soccer!

Contents

THE SCIENCE

Does science have much to do with soccer? You bet! Science affects everything. Why does a ball fall to the ground after you kick it in the air? Because of **gravity**. Understanding gravity is science. And understanding gravity helps you play better soccer.

[gravity – the force that attracts objects toward the center of Earth.]

THE SKILLS

Keepy Uppy

Beat gravity. Try keepy uppy! How long can you keep the ball in the air using your feet, thighs, body, and head?

Newton Helps Zink

The team decide Zink should start the game. They place the ball on the ground for him. Excited, Zink walks over to the ball. He stares at it. He waits. The ball just sits there.

THE SCIENCE

The ball won't move unless a **force** such as a kick, or gravity, or the **wind**, makes it move. Scientist Isaac Newton studied how and why things move. His three laws of motion help us understand movement in a scientific way.

Newton's First Law of Motion
"An object at rest remains at rest ... unless acted on by an **external** force."

THE SKILLS

Kicking

If your ankle wobbles, it is hard to control a kick. Lock your ankle by pointing your toes up. Then kick with the inside of your foot.

Kicking

Zink makes sure his ankle isn't wobbly. He gives the ball a little kick. It shuffles a short way ahead of him.

His teammates yell, "Kick it harder!" But how?

THE SCIENCE

A soccer ball is quite heavy, so a gentle kick without much force will not move the ball very far. A hard kick will move the ball farther and faster.

Newton's Second Law of Motion says that the greater the **mass** of an object, the more force it will take to accelerate the object.

THE SKILLS

Power kick

1. First, relax. Take a stride. Plant your non-kicking foot next to the ball, pointing where you want your kick to go.

2. Pull your kicking leg back. The further you bring this leg back the more power you'll have. Hold this V-shape.

3. Whip your knee, then your foot, forward. Strike the center of the ball with the knuckle of your big toe.

4. Watch your kick. Being bent over the ball gives the kick more power. Keep lifting your leg after you make contact.

Heading the Ball

Annie steps forward. She shows Zink how to do a powerful kick. The ball sails high into the air. As it hurtles back down, it hits Zink on the head. The ball bounces off the hard metal and spins away.

Newton's Third Law of Motion
"for every action in nature there is an equal and opposite reaction."

THE SCIENCE

As you kick, your foot exerts a force on the ball. At the same time, the ball exerts a force on your foot. You don't feel it because your leg has more mass and force than the ball. What if you kicked something with more mass, like a huge boulder? Your foot would feel the reaction then!

THE SKILLS

Headers

1. A ball may hurt you if it lands on the wrong part of your head. Practice doing headers using a foam ball, or a balloon.

2. Keep your eyes open, to make sure your forehead hits the ball. Keep your mouth closed. This tenses the head muscles, and keeps your jaw safe from stray elbows.

3. Rock backward. Then move your head forward using your whole body to create the force. Make forehead contact with the ball when your head is upright.

In the United States, soccer players age 10 and under are not allowed to head the ball for safety reasons.

Forces

Zink kicked the ball again. He watched it fly into the air. Zink had learned that gravity would pull the ball back down to the ground. But the ball didn't come straight down. It traveled along an **arc**.

Perhaps gravity isn't the only force acting on a soccer ball?

THE SCIENCE

Drag

Air pushes against the ball as it travels through it. This resistance is called **drag**. As the jumbled air reaches the back of the ball, it creates a messy area of air, which actually helps push the ball forward!

Lift

As the ball flies through the air, it pushes air downward. The air under it, in turn, pushes the ball upward in an equal and opposite reaction. This is known as **lift**.

THE SKILLS

Give the ball some lift

1. You can make the ball arc high in the air by getting your foot in the right position as you kick it.
2. Point your toes down to lock your ankle. To do a low kick you keep your toe pointing down. To lift the kick, bring your toes up as you kick.
3. The more you lift your toes, the more height you give the ball.

Wind

The force of the wind will affect how a ball travels through the air, too. A strong wind can move a soccer ball all by itself! You need to kick a lot harder if you kick against the wind.

Controlling the Ball

The ball landed far away, well out of Zink's reach. The team told Zink he needed to cushion the ball to control it. How do you do that?

THE SCIENCE

An object in motion stays in motion until a force acts on it. When a ball hits your body, you change its motion.

If a ball is traveling fast, your body will send it bouncing away fast. To control the ball, you need to slow it as it reaches you. How? You need to cushion the ball.

Try this. Ask if you can use an egg, then head outside. Throw and catch the egg—but remember—if your hands keep still, the egg will usually break.

Instead, as you catch it, move your hands in the direction the egg is traveling. This gradually slows the egg, so it won't break. That's cushioning!

THE SKILLS

Cushioning

1. To cushion the ball with your foot, move your foot slightly back to absorb the impact.

2. Control a high ball with your chest. With feet shoulder-width apart, lean back slightly as the ball hits your chest. The ball should drop at your feet, ready for you to kick.

3. You can cushion the ball with your thigh, too. Lift your leg and angle your thigh down 45 degrees. Just as the ball is about to land, pull your thigh back a little.

Bendy Like a Banana

James wants to practice his free kicks. The team put Zink in goal. Some of the team stand in a line in front of the goal posts, ready to jump. Zink relaxes, he feels pretty sure the ball won't reach him. But James has some pretty fancy skills!

THE SCIENCE

German scientist Gustav Magnus studied why cannonballs curved in flight. Now called the **Magnus force**, curved flight happens because air travels faster on the edge of the ball that spins in the direction the ball is traveling. Air travels slower on the other edge. This imbalance causes the ball to curve.

Experiment with Magnus force. Roll some paper into a cylinder. Hold a large book in midair at a 45-degree angle. Roll the cylinder down the book. Watch the cylinder as it falls off the end. The spin should curve it back under the book.

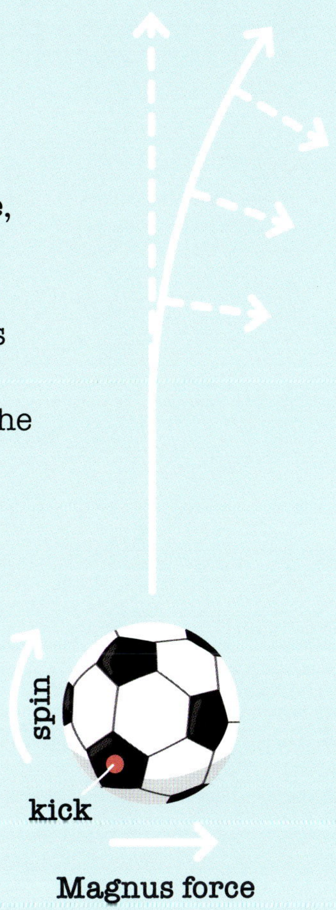

THE SKILLS

How to kick a curve ball

Kick the ball hard, near the bottom, at one side. The ball will rise up and spin. At first the ball will travel in the direction of the kick. As the ball slows, the spinning causes one side of the ball to move faster than the other side, making the ball curve. Kick the right side of the ball to bend it left, the left side to bend it right.

Balancing Tricks

Zink swung his right leg and gave the ball a huge kick. So huge, he fell over! Zink is not very good at standing on one leg. You need great balance to play soccer.

THE SCIENCE

We use our eyes and ears and body senses to help us balance. Our bodies are always adjusting, and working, to keep balanced. Try standing on one leg with your eyes closed. Your body will wobble around, working hard to stay still.

THE SKILLS

Training balance

Balance pads help develop good balance. You can use a thick pillow or cushion instead. The wobbly surface forces you to use small muscles you don't usually use.

Make the area around you safe. Then stand on a cushion on one leg. Try moving your other leg forward, backward, and to each side. Try raising your arms. and lean forward, backward, and sideways.

Throw-ins

The ball left the pitch, or field. The team ask Zink to throw the ball in. They tell him to stand with both feet behind the touch line, where the ball went out. He has to throw the ball a long way to reach his teammates.

THE SKILLS

Good throw-ins

1. Hold the ball behind your head, with your hands behind the ball and fingers spread.
2. Relax your arms and bend your elbows. Stand with feet shoulder-width apart. Keep your feet behind the sideline.
3. Lean back, bend your knees a little, and arch your body. Scan the field to decide who to throw to.
4. Propel your body and arms forward. Let go of the ball as it goes over your head.

Remember to keep both feet behind the line!

THE SCIENCE

A good throw-in needs **momentum**. Momentum is the strength or force that something has when it is moving.

A heavy object has more momentum than a light object. An object traveling fast has more force than a slow one.

A soccer ball's mass (how heavy it is) is the same no matter how you throw it. To increase its momentum, you need to increase its speed.

Stepping forward as you throw adds momentum. Or, create momentum by arching your body and flicking the ball forward as you release the ball.

Soccer Balls

Zink picked up a soccer ball and looked at it. It appeared to be made out of lots of six-sided pieces, joined together. He wondered how it was made and what it was made from.

1 First, two or three layers of cloth backing are glued and pressed to sheets of synthetic leather.

2 A machine cuts the sheets into hexagons and punches the stitch holes.

3 Most balls have a design or logo on them. This is printed onto the hexagons, using a special fast-drying paint.

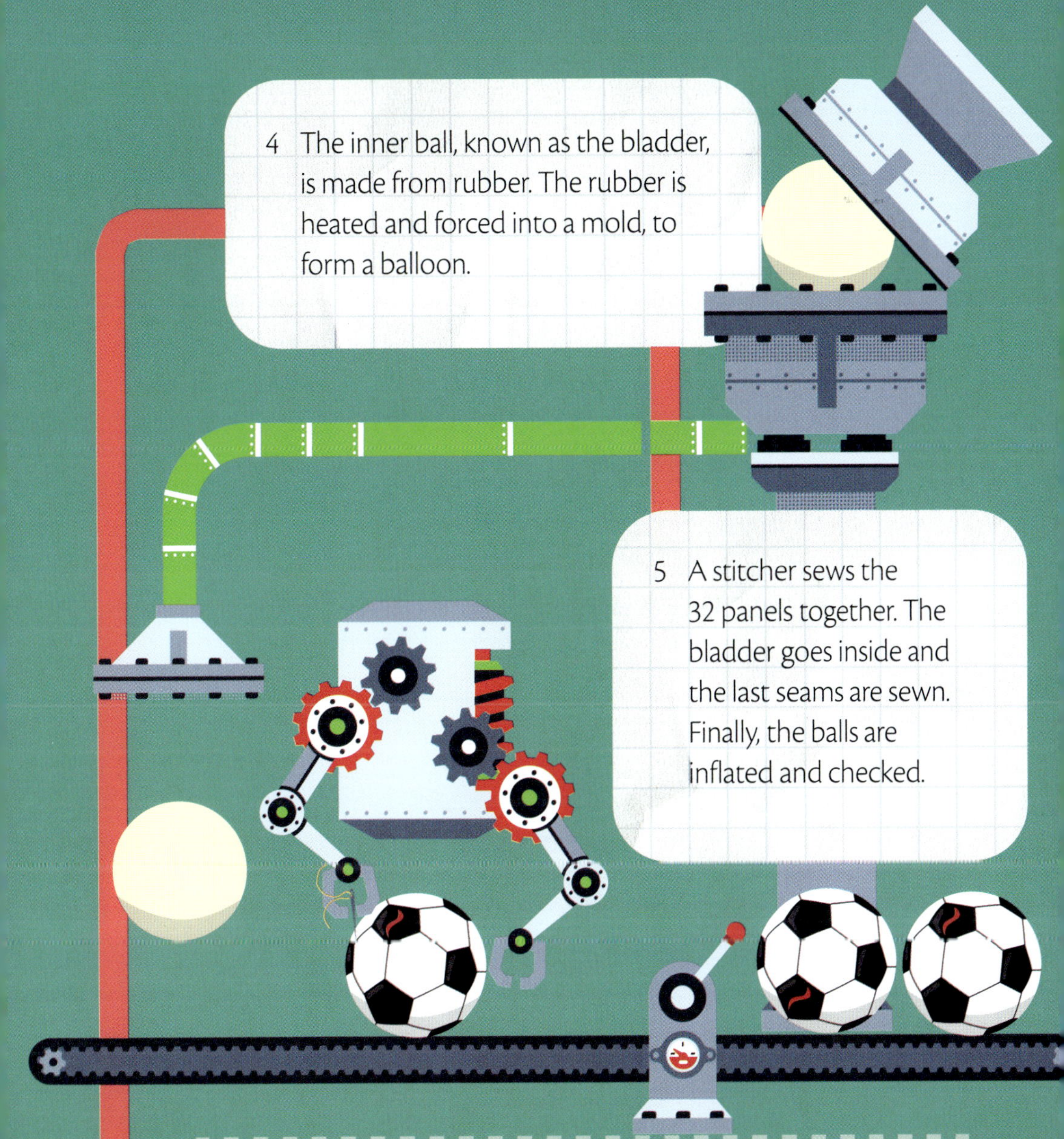

4 The inner ball, known as the bladder, is made from rubber. The rubber is heated and forced into a mold, to form a balloon.

5 A stitcher sews the 32 panels together. The bladder goes inside and the last seams are sewn. Finally, the balls are inflated and checked.

THE SCIENCE

Making soccer balls takes some science knowledge. Scientists test different **materials** to decide which would make the best balls. Tiny changes to the surface, the stitches, or the weight of a ball make a big difference in how it will behave when it is kicked or thrown.

Friction on the Pitch

The pitch plays an important part in a game of soccer. Zink's pitch is grass, but some are made from **artificial** turf. Indoor soccer is often played on turf too. Each surface make the ball behave differently.

THE SCIENCE

Friction is when one surface or object rubs against another. Friction works in the opposite direction to the direction the object is moving. When a soccer ball hits the ground, friction slows the ball down.

Try to push, not roll, a ball along the grass and feel the friction.

No one wants to stop the ball more than the goalkeeper! Friction helps the goalkeeper hold onto the ball.

Goalkeeper gloves have a surface that creates more friction. Rubber or foam on the palms help cushion the ball, too.

THE SKILLS

Goalkeeping

1. Stand with your feet shoulder-width apart. Hold your hands up, with fingers open. Lean forward with your knees slightly bent.

2. Practice side-stepping left to right in this position along the goal mouth.

3. As the ball approaches, turn your lower body sideways and kneel on one knee. Your leg makes a barrier in case the ball goes through your hands.

4. With fingers pointing to the ground, pick up the ball and pull it to your chest.

Dribbling

Zink wants to try dribbling. Dribbling is when you nudge the ball just ahead of you as you run around the pitch. It's a very important skill.

THE SKILLS

Dribbling the ball

1. Keep your head up to scan the pitch.

2. Practice dribbling around some markers, using both feet, and both sides of your feet. Keep the ball close.

3. Keep moving and changing speed. Being unpredictable makes it hard for anyone to steal the ball.

4. Use your body to shield the ball from opponents.

5. Try doing turns. Put your foot on top of the ball and drag it backward. Spin on your other foot and move off in the other direction.

6. Confuse your opponents. Fake taking a kick, but then step over the ball instead.

THE SCIENCE

Are shorter players better dribblers? Usually, yes. Why? Because of their low **center of gravity**. Gravity pulls objects toward Earth's center. Zink's head is heavy, so there is more mass above his waist than below it.

If Zink leans over too far, gravity pulls the top of his body and he will topple over. The lower your center of gravity, the easier it is to keep your balance.

Try it. Sit on a chair opposite a mirror. When sitting you have a low center of gravity. Lean left as far as you can. Now stand up and try to lean as far.

Zink's center of gravity is above his waist.

A soccer ball's center of gravity is at its center.

Build a Soccer Body

To play well, you need be fit. You can train your **muscles** to become stronger. Zink's whole body has worked hard today!

THE SCIENCE

The more you use your muscles, the stronger they get. Even eye muscles!

Zink's eyes send signals to his brain. His brain tells his body what to do.

Goalkeeping needs strong, grippy hands.

A strong neck helps Zink head the ball.

Arms and shoulders help Zink throw, and balance, too.

Zink's core supports him and helps him balance.

Strong thigh muscles help Zink run faster and give his kicks more power.

Zink's lower leg helps him run and controls his foot.

THE SKILLS

Body training

Build up slowly. Don't do an exercise if it feels uncomfortable.

1. Train your eyes! Place an object on a table in front of you. Put a cup with a straw in it off to one side. Try to put a toothpick in the straw, while staring at your object. This trains your eyes to see areas away from the ball.

2. Do crunches to strengthen your core and neck. Lie on your back and bring your knees toward your chest. At the same time, gently raise your head toward your knees.

3. For leg and arm strength, squat down with the ball, then jump up and push the ball up as high as you can. Squat back down and do it again.

4. To strengthen your hands and wrists try passing the ball back and forth from one hand to another as quietly as possible. If you hear a slap, it means you are not cushioning the pass.

Soccer Science Quiz

Do you have soccer science know-how? See if you can answer these questions. The answers are on page 32.

1. What force pulls a flying ball back down to the ground?
   a) lift   b) gravity   c) friction

2. What effect does Magnus force have on a kick?
   a) it causes it to curve   b) it stops the ball
   c) it makes the ball heavier

3. Which kick has more momentum, a gentle kick, or a hard kick?

4. What force slows a ball down when it rolls along the grass?
   a) gravity   b) drag   c) friction

Science words

arc a curving path.

artificial made by human beings rather than occurring naturally.

center of gravity the point in an object or person where their weight is balanced.

drag a force acting opposite to the motion of any object moving.

external occurring outside.

force a push or a pull.

friction the resistance a surface or object encounters when sliding over another.

gravity the force that pulls things toward the center of Earth.

lift an upward-acting force.

Magnus force a lift force that acts on a spinning object.

mass how much matter is in an object.

material the matter something is made from.

momentum the strength of a moving object.

muscle tissue in the body of animals and humans that moves parts of the body.

wind the movement of air near Earth's surface.

Index

Quiz answers: 1. b) gravity; 2. a) it causes it to curve; 3. a hard kick; 4. c) friction